Dear Charlie,

A Grandfather's Love Letter

A Guide to Your Life with Autism

Earle P. Martin, Jr.

Foreword by Gary B. Mesibov, Ph.D.

Dedication

I dedicate this book to my wonderful grandson
and best friend, Charlie Stubbs.

Earle Martin

Foreword

It is a treat for me to introduce this delightful book by a very special person. I met the author, Earle Martin, several years ago, and he immediately became one of my favorite people. A grandfather of a young man with autism, Earle originally contacted me to help evaluate and make recommendations for the grandson he cherished, Charlie. I was instantly impressed by Earle and Charlie's mom and dad during our initial contact, and my admiration for all of them only grows with each passing day. Not only are they committed and devoted to providing Charlie with the best possible opportunity for a full and rich life, they also show a unique understanding of their youngster and have made an unrelenting commitment to help him become the best person he can be.

Although the family is dedicated to facilitating Charlie's progress, and he has made enormous strides forward since we first met, the family still respects who he is and does not want, or expect, Charlie to give up any of his personal identity or uniqueness.

Earle's understanding of, and respect for, his grandson is evident throughout this book, and that is what makes it so special. The book started as a personal message for Charlie, answering all the questions his grandfather thought his grandson might ask, just in case Earle would not be around when all of these questions arose. Earle's sensitivity, humanity, and insight are evident in his choice of topics to discuss and the wonderfully concrete, yet comprehensive, answers he offers for some very complex questions. Earle's talent for probing profound questions with insight and the concreteness that autism requires is evident throughout the book.

Future Horizons, Inc.

When Charlie's parents and I read early drafts of this wonderful book, we urged Earle to make it available to a larger audience beyond his grandson. Earle agreed to do this, and the following is the product that evolved. I am delighted that Earle has agreed to share his wisdom and understanding so generously so that others might benefit from his very important messages.

This book is Earle's work, but Charlie's mom and dad have been very involved with reading, re-reading, editing, and suggesting. I think that this is appropriate in this situation because the book reflects the same teamwork that this remarkable family has shown in raising such a delightful, spirited, and charming young man with autism. Through this book, the collective wisdom of Earle's clan is now a treasure that can be shared.

This contribution will help the people with autism, the target audience. Parents, family members, and other individuals will also find these humane insights to be poignant, thought provoking, and inspiring. It has been rare in my experience to meet a man as sincere, forthright, and humane as Earle, and this very special book reflects all of these wonderful attributes. I know you will enjoy reading this book as much as I have.

Gary B. Mesibov, Ph.D.
Professor and Director
Division TEACCH
University of North Carolina
at Chapel Hill

Acknowledgments

I thank Charlie's mom and dad, Melinda and Sam Stubbs, for their encouragement and insightful suggestions in helping me write this book. We have spent many hours over the years in our coming to know and respect Charlie. Even as I have learned so much from Charlie, so too have I learned so much from them. They are far more central and important in Charlie's life than I am, and so much of his liking himself and his growth are the results of their love and devotion.

This book started as a letter to Charlie and then grew into a book. I sent it to Gary Mesibov of Division TEACCH and asked him to review it and make sure I was not misleading Charlie about his autism. We hold Gary in the highest esteem and have consistently found him to be a kind source of strength (and worthy of our trust). He knows autism, and he knows Charlie. In the midst of a world of sometimes-loud voices and claims, his is a calm voice, and his only claim is that he wants to help both Charlie and us.

For us, as for so many others, Gary does that very well. It was Gary who suggested that I widen the scope of the book to not only help Charlie, but also help others touched by autism. He made a number of helpful suggestions and worked with me as I tried to incorporate them. Thank you, Gary, for your invaluable help with the book and especially for your help with Charlie.

My thanks to Wayne Gilpin and Polly McGlew of Future Horizons for recognizing in this book the potential for helping people with autism and those who care so much about them. I thank Wayne and Polly for their excellent suggestions in how best to present the book—and specifically thank Polly for her dedicated hours of thoughtful and skillful editing—resulting in a better book for all those whom may be helped by it.

Finally, I wish to thank all those who have loved Charlie and have been loved by him. They have helped him grow, and they have also grown because of Charlie

Earle Martin

I am Charlie.

I like myself.

I am glad that I am Charlie.

Future Horizons, Inc.

Table of Contents

Future Horizons, Inc.

Chapter One
To Begin

For a better feeling for, and an understanding of, autism.

Charlie, what I have written to you won't tell you everything about autism, but I hope that what you read here will give you a better feel for your autism.

All people with autism have some things that are alike, and they also have many things that make them different from each other. As you get older and come to know yourself better than anyone else can know you, you will see just how autism applies to you.

Talk with your mom and dad about what you read here, and you can talk with them about your questions, thoughts, and feelings about learning that you have autism. Not only do they love you so much (and are very proud of you), but they also know so much that can help you.

I hope that you will also talk with me about your autism. I would be very glad to talk with you.

There are professionals in the field of autism to whom you can talk. Not all of them will be helpful, but some of them are quite good. Among those who can be helpful are a man named Gary Mesibov and a woman named Kaia Mates, both of whom you know, and who are our friends. They and their friends at Division TEACCH at the University of North Carolina at Chapel Hill can give you much help.

There are also books and newsletters on autism that you can read. Not all of them will be helpful, but some of them are quite good.

I hope you will read Temple Grandin's books. Dr. Grandin is a woman who has autism. She teaches at Colorado State University in Fort Collins, Colorado—not far from Estes Park, where you and your family take vacations.

I also hope you will read Susan Moreno's newsletter. She has a daughter who has autism, and she is editor of a newsletter called "The MAPP." Susan Moreno ends each newsletter by saying, "You are not alone."

Charlie, you are not alone! You have those of us who know you well and love you so much. You have others who are there to help you. Your journey in life with autism is yours, but I hope that you will seek and accept real help along the way.

Charlie, what I have written is a guidebook for living your life with autism. I think that living your life with autism is a challenge. I hope that this guidebook will help you win that challenge.

By using the word "challenge," I mean something that is not easy to do. A challenge takes work to meet it the best way you can. Your effort and the right skills can enable you to meet the challenge. I think living your life with autism is a challenge.

When you meet the challenge the best way that you can, you win. When you meet the challenge the best way that you can, you feel good.

Future Horizons, Inc.

Live your life to the fullest. I am convinced that this is a challenge you can accept and win! This will not be easy and will take work, but you can do it!

Any challenge will call for your understanding and effort. It will call for your learning and using the skills that will help you. Then, you can win the challenge of living your life with autism.

You will read more about seeing autism as a challenge in Chapter Fifteen. I look at this guidebook like a guidebook to one of your Nintendo games. I have seen you carefully study the Nintendo guidebooks before you play your games, and I have seen you open them up and study them again. Study the guidebook and play the game.

I hope that you will use this guidebook in the same way. Study and then live your life with autism.

One more thing—I hope that you will also write a guidebook for living with autism. You will know better than anyone else, including me, what it is like to live with autism. You will know what works and what doesn't. This will help you live your life the best way you can.

I would love to read what you write!

Chapter Two
What Is Autism?

Thoughts on a definition.

"Autism" is a noun, and "autistic" is an adjective. A person who has autism is autistic. If you, or others who know you, look up autism in the dictionary, this is what you or they will probably find: "Autism... a state of mind characterized by daydreaming, hallucinations, and disregard of external reality."

While dictionaries are helpful for the meaning of many words, this definition is not accurate. My dictionary is the most recent I could find (Webster's New World College Dictionary, Third Edition, 1997), but even it has an old definition that isn't correct.

What most dictionaries' definitions say is not true about autism as we now know it to be. And it is certainly not true for your autism!

The best definition of autism that I have found is one I just read in a book entitled, *Autism, Understanding the Disorder*, by Gary Mesibov, Lynn Adams and Laura Klinger. They wrote:

> *Today we understand autism as a neurobiological condition that affects how people perceive and understand the world."*

I think that definition puts it very well. Autism is a neurobiological condition. "Neuro" means that it has to do with our brains. "Bio" means that it has to do with our bodies. A "condition" is what autism is. Autism is caused by a few differences in your brain. It affects how you perceive (or see) and understand the world.

Read through the words yet to come. Talk with your mom, dad, and others. Think about your own thoughts and feelings.

As you do these things, I believe that you will get a better idea about your autism.

Future Horizons, Inc.

Chapter Three
What Having Autism Means and Doesn't Mean

What it is and is not.

Having autism means that your brain operates differently in the ways it understands and responds to other people and the environment. Having autism is not your fault. It just happens because of the way a small part of your brain operates. You didn't do anything to cause that small part of your brain to operate that way.

Having autism is nothing to be ashamed of and nothing to hide or pretend isn't there. Autism doesn't mean that you are bad or not as good as other boys and girls. Charlie, you are a very good boy, as fine as any child could ever be!

Regardless of the dictionary definition, having autism doesn't mean that you are crazy or mentally ill. Charlie, you are sane, which means that you are mentally healthy! Autism doesn't mean that you are stupid, dumb or retarded. While some people with autism are retarded, you are not.

Your intelligence has been tested by some of the best intelligence testers in the country, and they found you have normal intelligence. In some ways, I think you are above normal. You have what is described as high-functioning autism.

It isn't that you are a better or worse person than someone who is not autistic, but it is simply that your brain operates differently in the ways it understands and responds to other people and the environment. And it isn't that you are a better or worse person than someone else who has autism but is retarded. Your brain is just more able than his or hers to understand some things. You can be grateful for not being retarded, but I hope you will always respect and be kind to those people who are retarded.

Future Horizons, Inc.

Chapter Four
What Does It Mean for You To Be Autistic?

Why I feel different; a few differences in my brain.

I think being autistic means that you sometimes feel different from other boys and girls. You might feel that other children seem to understand things that you don't understand. Other boys and girls may seem to understand each other, but they don't understand you, and you may not understand them.

Do you wonder why other boys and girls seem to talk and play together so easily when it is so hard for you to do the same? They don't seem to know how to play your games the way you want them to, and sometimes you can't figure out how to play their games the way they want you to.

Other children may know just what to say, but you have to work so hard deciding what to say. The boys and girls may seem to be able to understand the meaning of a certain look or phrase that doesn't mean to you what it means to them.

Because of all this, you might feel left out. Do you think that the other children speak one language and you speak another? You might feel that they are all on one planet and you are on a different one. The children could seem to be together, and you feel apart. You might feel that you don't fit in.

Why do you feel different from other boys and girls in these ways? The answer is that there are a few differences in your brain that make it especially hard for you to understand things like they do, talk and play as they do, and just know what to say.

In these few ways, the other children's brains work differently from yours; therefore, you sometimes have a hard time understanding them, just as they sometimes have a hard time understanding you. Also, because of those few differences in your brain and their brains, you are more likely than they are to give all of your attention to something in your mind or imagination. This might be a tape you have watched or something you have read. You have a real power of concentration, and when you concentrate on a subject, you seem to block out those around you.

That's why you will occasionally hear us say, "Charlie, where is what you are doing from? What tape is it from?" And, sometimes we will say, "Charlie! Charlie! This isn't the time to play a tape in your mind!"

With your powers of concentration, you are completely focused on the tape or whatever else is on your mind, and your brain doesn't have the skill to hide what you are doing from others around you.

The few differences in your brain, the way you concentrate on something, are different from a lot of people in two ways. First, your powers of concentration are greater than most people's. Second, you don't have the natural ability to hide what you are thinking about from others around you. Other people think about other things too, such as tapes and games, but they have a greater ability to hide that from the people around them.

Future Horizons, Inc.

A few differences in your brain and their brains. That's it. This is why you feel different from other people. That's what it means for you to have autism.

Chapter Five
Our Brains

Using other parts of my brain.

Each person has a brain, which is one of the body's most important organs. The brain is located in each person's head.

The brain is the organ where our thoughts take place—where we do our thinking. It is where we take in what we sense around us and respond to it. We record in our brains what we see, hear and feel. We keep facts and ideas we have learned in our brains.

Here are two examples of how I think your brain works. First, when you read one of your Nintendo maps, you understand what to do when you play the game. Not only do you understand what to do, you can also then do it. You direct your thumbs on your remote control to go to the right places (with the correct timing). Your brain is very good at that, while many other people can't do that well with their brains.

Second, when people say something to you, you don't just automatically know what to say back to them. This is an area where your brain is different from most other people's. You have to use another part of your brain to decide what you could say, and then you say it.

Because your brain doesn't easily know what to answer the other person, you choose to use another part of your brain to decide what to answer.

The first example is in an area where your brain can do things most of us don't do very well. The second example is in an area where part of your brain doesn't function as well as most other people's brains. That's the autistic part of your brain.

What do you do? The answer is to use and develop that part of your brain that works well and learn how to use other parts of your brain to make up for what the autistic part of your brain doesn't do well.

Chapter Six
Accepting Your Autism

Yes, I have autism. I am autistic.

To accept that you have autism means that you say, "Yes, I have autism. I am autistic." It's like saying, "Yes, I have two eyes. I am a two-eyed person." You accept that you have two eyes, and you accept that you have autism.

Accepting that you have autism isn't as easy as accepting that you have two eyes. You can look in the mirror and see that you have two eyes, but you can't look in the mirror and see that you have autism. For now, I am asking you to take my word for it, and your mom and dad are asking that you take their word for it. To accept autism for now means to act as if it were so.

When I first heard that you had autism, I didn't know what autism was. I didn't know anything about autism, and this scared me.

I knew that it was a "disability," which meant that in some way you were disabled from understanding things the way most people do. Once I really learned about autism, and especially how it applied to you, I wasn't afraid of it anymore. Once I learned its "abilities," and what you could do with it, I could easily accept autism.

Autism is not an enemy (like a Donkey Kong boss) whom you may fear and have to fight or run from.

To accept that you have autism is to say that it is there. It's part of you. It isn't Charlie; it's just a small part of

Charlie. Autism isn't the whole you, but just a small part of you.

Recognize autism's limits and strengths. Find other ways around its limits by using other parts of your brain. And, as for autism's strengths, learn them and build on them.

Chapter Seven
Telling Others about You and Asking about Them

Knowing each other better.

Most of us would like for others to know about us—who we are, how we feel, and what we think. Many of us would like to know these things about others around us.

Sometimes, we think that others know us. We think they can just tell about us without our having to tell them. We think that our tone of voice, the look on our faces, and whether we are smiling or frowning should be enough for them to know us. But it isn't.

Occasionally, we think we know others. We hear their tone of voice, see the look on their faces, see a smile or frown, and decide that we know them. We don't.

Just because we see things a certain way, we might think that others see things the same way. They might not.

We feel a certain way, so we think that other people feel the same way. They might not feel the same.

The truth is, while we are the same as other people in so many ways, we differ in other ways. We feel and think differently about certain things.

Therefore, we can't "just tell" what a person is thinking or feeling. We can't really know another person by a tone of voice, a look on a face, or a smile or frown.

We all have trouble knowing another person and what he or she thinks. We have trouble knowing that another person may see things differently than we do.

Some people who know a lot about autism think that autistic people have even more trouble with this than the rest of us. People with autism have more trouble knowing another person and what he or she feels or thinks. They have trouble recognizing that another person may see things differently than they do.

We all have to work hard at knowing another person. Because of your autism, I think you have to work even harder to know another person.

What can you do to know people better? The answer is that you ask them about themselves. Ask what they are thinking, what they are feeling, how they see things, and what is their point of view. See what they like to do; such as what are their favorite books, Nintendo games, or computer games.

You ask, and then you listen. Try hard to listen to what other people tell you. In this way, you can know them better.

How about other people knowing you better? They can ask about you, and you can answer them. Then, they will know you better.

What if people don't ask about you? What do you do then? The answer is that you can tell them about you.

Tell them about what you are thinking and how you are feeling. Talk about how you see things and what your

Future Horizons, Inc.

favorite things are. Describe what you like to do—playing Nintendo, listening to music, swimming, etc.

You can tell people about your cats and about Andrew and your mom and dad. Tell people about Dell and Amanda.

You are getting so much better about asking another person about himself or herself and telling that person about you. If you see me writing something, you ask me what I am writing. You are more aware when I don't understand something that you understand. I couldn't see the lights in the "Base Launch Zone." You tried to show me several times, but I still didn't understand. So, you said, "You just don't get it, do you?" You were right; I didn't get it. You understood. You tried to tell me about the lights.

You tell me when I hurt your feelings. You told me that I hurt your feelings when I laughed at the "Figure it Out" panel members when slime was poured on them.

You ask others about them. You tell others about you.

Another thought, Charlie. You could tell some people about what it is like to have autism. Whom can you tell? I think you may tell those people whom you like and trust, and whom you want to really know you better.

How and when do you tell them? You should talk to your mom and dad. If they aren't available, talk to one of your brothers or sister. If they aren't around, talk to a trusted friend who knows that you have autism.

Telling another person about your autism can be a difficult social interaction. Your mom and dad or a trusted friend who already knows you have autism can be very helpful in just how to go about that social interaction. That person might also agree to be with you when you try to tell another person about your autism.

Future Horizons, Inc.

Chapter Eight
Being Different

We are all different.
Telling others about my autistic differences.

We are all different from each other, no matter whom we are. Just as you feel different from other boys and girls in some ways, each of them also feels different from each other. Even those boys and girls who seem to have such an easy time talking and playing together sometimes feel different and apart from each other.

One difference is that some of us are boys and others are girls. We can be either tall or short. Some of us have blue eyes, and others have brown eyes. People can be handsome or pretty, but other people are plain. Some people are very good at certain subjects, like math or reading, but others are not. There are those that are popular with other children, but many are not.

Some differences are easy to see. We can usually tell if someone is black, white, brown, or oriental. We figure out that someone is thin or fat. If someone is a boy or a girl, we know the difference. We can see that someone wears glasses. Some differences are harder to tell, but we can learn to see them when we are given some clues and give it some thought.

If we watch "Figure it Out - Family Style" and see a person with a seeing-eye dog or a long, white cane that he or she moves in front, those clues help us figure out that he or she can't see—this person is blind.

When we see a person who wears hearing aids in one or both ears, or uses sign language, these are clues that help us figure out that this person has difficulty hearing (or is deaf). A person who has to use a wheelchair to move from one place to another shows us that he or she either can't walk or finds walking very hard or painful.

Some differences are more difficult to understand than being blind, deaf, or unable to walk. The clues are harder to figure out. Autism is one of those differences.

With little thought, most people can see a seeing-eye-dog or a white cane, and then tell that someone is blind. They can see someone using sign language or hearing aids and then figure out that person is deaf or hard-of-hearing.

Most people can see someone in a wheelchair and know that the person either can't walk or can't walk without pain. However, most people don't know much, if anything, about autism. Because there are no clues as clear as a seeing-eye dog, a cane, hearing aids, sign language, or a wheelchair, it's hard for people to tell if someone is autistic.

So, we have to tell them about autism. We have to teach them about what it's like being autistic and help them figure out how you are different.

As you get older, I hope that you also teach people. If we don't tell them, if you don't tell them, then we can't expect them to understand how and why you are different. (Please read again the last section of Chapter Seven before you try to tell someone about your autism.)

Some people you tell about your autism still won't understand. A few won't care. Some people will be afraid of anyone or anything different from them and won't want to understand.

However, there will be some people who, once they understand the differences and have figured out the mystery of how and why you are different, may see not only how you are different, but also how you are the same as they are.

These people will trade their confusion about you for a feeling of knowing you. They will be better able to see you as you really are. They will be better able to see your courage and your work to live successfully in a world of people who are mostly not autistic.

You will know these people better than you had before. You will see a part of them that you may have missed. Both they and you will feel better about yourselves and can be better friends.

Chapter Nine
Time Alone and Time with Others

Why I need both.

I think every person needs to spend some time alone and some time with other people. I know that I do, and I think it is important for you.

I try to spend the first hour or two of each day alone, and from time-to-time during the day, I try to be alone again, even if it is only for a little while. I then try to be with other people—to socially interact with them. Time alone and time with others is healthy.

As I said earlier, the part of your brain that makes it easy to socially interact with other people works in a different way with people without autism. It's harder for you to socially interact with others. Because it is harder to socially interact, I think you may want to spend **too** much time alone. And when you are with others, you may want to ignore them.

On the other hand, you may not want to seem different from others. You may enjoy being with others more than you think. Therefore, you could try to spend too much time with them and not enough time by yourself.

I think you need to do both—spend time with others and spend time alone. You need to spend time with others, using and practicing your social skills and experiencing the good things that come from interacting with people.

You have already experienced some of the good things that come from interacting with people. You interact with your mom and dad; Andrew, Max, and Whitney; Grandpa Jack and Grandma Dotty; and Nanny and me. You also have interacted with your cousins and with Mrs. Selby and Mrs. Kroeger. You socialize with your friends at school and with many others whom you know and who know you.

You have talked to them and listened to them. They have talked to you and listened to you. All of you have learned from each other; all of you have had fun.

These are just some of the good things that can come from using your social skills and interacting with others. However, you also need to spend time alone. Experience the rest and relaxation that can come from your taking breaks from the work of social interaction. Take time to do just what you want to do. Time alone with yourself helps you get your bearings and know yourself.

Some of the great men of history have spent time alone and with others. One such man was Gandhi, who lived in the country of India when I was a boy. He was one of the most important people of the twentieth century. Gandhi spent the first four hours of each day alone and the rest of the day with other people.

Another man was Gautama, the first Buddha (which means "Enlightened One"), on whom the Buddhist religion is based. He spent the first half of every day alone and then the rest of the day with other people.

These men realized that they needed to be alone and then with others. I tell you about Gandhi and Gautama as a way

Future Horizons, Inc.

of saying how important it is to spend time both alone and with others.

I think it is easier for you to be alone. I think it is harder for you to be with other people. Easier or harder, I think you can do both.

Chapter Ten
Mistakes

It's O.K. to make mistakes.

Charlie, I know that you don't like to make mistakes. Neither do I. But, both of us, and everyone else, make mistakes. That's O.K.

I have read that many people with autism don't like to make mistakes. They seem to think that whatever they do must be done perfectly.

Sometimes, people with autism will not want to try something new because they are afraid that they might make mistakes. They miss out on some really good things because they are afraid that they cannot do them perfectly.

Charlie, we all make mistakes—there is no getting around it. Mistakes are a part of living, and that's O.K. There is no shame in making mistakes. I am sixty-six-years old, and I think that I have made more than sixty-six thousand mistakes.

A student could answer a math problem incorrectly. People might talk when they are not supposed to. We could line up in the wrong place in line.

I made a mistake when I kept saying, "Dark Vader." You helped me get it right, asking me to look at you and then making the "th" sound for me to see and hear. Then, I could get it right. I could say, "Darth Vader."

Sometimes, when you play the piano, you will say, "Pots, we are in trouble. I made a mistake." You keep trying to play it right. Most of the time you quickly succeed in getting it right. At other times, you say, "I can't get it right now. I will try later."

You try to guess the answer to the bonus question on "Wheel of Fortune." I've heard you guess it correctly. When you don't guess it correctly, I've heard you say, "I was so close!" You repeat the right answer and say it aloud. You've learned something new.

Mistakes have value. We learn from them. We learn what to do and what not to do. If we didn't make mistakes, we could never learn what to do or not do.

Sure, there are some mistakes that we need to try very hard not to make. These are mistakes that might hurt someone, such as a person going to sleep while driving a car, or a doctor removing the wrong organ from someone's body. These are deadly serious mistakes.

Most mistakes aren't like that. Most of our mistakes don't hurt anyone. The worst they do is just embarrass us or make us angry.

Charlie, while I know that you don't like to make mistakes, I also know that you have made wonderful progress in your willingness to accept your mistakes. They don't upset you nearly as much as they used to.

I hope that you will keep up the good work. Try new things that look worth trying. If they look worth trying, then they are worth risking making mistakes.

Future Horizons, Inc.

Chapter Eleven
Friends

Liking myself and being liked by others.

People are always talking about friends. "He is my friend." "She is my friend." "They are friends." "Who are your friends?"

Just what is a friend? I think a friend is someone you know and like. You like a person because that person is nice to you or helps you. Perhaps you like a person because he or she shares with you.

A person might be a friend because you both like to do the same things. You might like certain people because you can talk to them and they will listen to you.

Someone could like you for some of the same reasons: you are nice, you help, or you share. The other reasons could be that you both like to do the same things or because you listen to that person.

Sometimes a boy or girl will say, "I have lots of friends," or, "I don't have many friends," or even, "I don't have any friends." When I look around me, I find that most people have some friends. Some have a lot of friends, but most have just a few friends.

The people who have only a few friends need to know that it's that way for most people. Having only a few friends doesn't mean that there is anything wrong. In fact, I think that we are pretty lucky to have a few friends. We can be glad for that and really enjoy the friends we have. What's most important is that we like ourselves, and that each of us is his or her own friend.

I remember a book entitled, *How to be Your Own Best Friend*, that talked about how people can be their own friends. This book describes how we can be someone we both know and like.

Once we like ourselves, we can reach out to others. We may end up making friends with some of them.

What do you do to make a friend? Well, you can be nice to someone, such as when you call a person by name. You can write on a schoolmate's math paper, "Good job!," when the work is done right, or, "Almost got it, keep trying!" if he or she made a mistake.

You can help someone, such as when you help a new classmate learn what to do at your school, or when you help a younger child take a nap by gently patting him or her on the back. You can share, like the time you took Andrew a Gatorade at his baseball game.

Find things to do with people. Do things with someone that are fun for you and might be fun for the other boy or girl. You could play videogames with someone, or you could ask your mom to take both of you to McDonald's or IHOP.

Talk to a person about what you like to do. Tell about what's fun for you at your lake house. Talk about a CD-ROM you especially like. Describe a fun television show. You can even talk about your cats.

Listen to the other person. You can listen to what someone did that was fun. Pay attention when someone tells you

Future Horizons, Inc.

about a pet, book, or television show he or she likes. Listen to what the other person wants to tell you.

And you can smile. That can be a big help in perhaps making a friend. See what happens. Sometimes you will make a friend; sometimes not.

I hope you enjoy the friends you make. If you try to be someone's friend, and he or she doesn't want to be friends, that is okay. You will have other friends.

One caution is to be careful. Don't do anything that you don't think is right in order to make a friend. Don't try to please other people by doing things you really don't want to do just to get them to like you. You won't like yourself for doing something you didn't think was right, and the friend won't be worth having.

Charlie, you have friends now: your mom and dad, Andrew, Max, Whitney, Grandma Dotty, Grandpa Jack, Nanny, Dell. Amanda, Jolie, and me.

Mrs. Selby and Mrs. Kroeger, your teachers, are also your friends. You have schoolmates who are your friends. Coda, Bianca, Becky, Angie and Nicole are your friends. You have friends in your Cub Scout Bear Den. Peter, John, and Braden are friends of yours.

There are four other wonderful friends—your cats, Steve and Doug, and your dogs, Sassy and Maggie. While Sassy has died and gone to live with God, she is still a friend. Maggie has moved to the farm, but she is also your friend.

Someone once said that a dog is man's best friend. I think that is true. For a man or woman, or a boy or girl, dogs are wonderful friends. I have never had a cat, but I would have to say that your cats are wonderful friends, too.

By the time you read this, some of us, like your dog Sassy, may have died and gone to be with God in Heaven. Others may have just moved away. But, we are all still your friends, and you are our friend.

Others will become your friends as you grow older, and I believe that anyone who becomes your friend will be glad. I think you will be glad, too.

Future Horizons, Inc.

Chapter Twelve
What You Might Be

I follow my interests. I follow my dreams. I get help along the way. I let people whom I trust teach me, but I make my own decisions.

Have you ever wondered what you might be when you grow up? What kind of a job you might have? What you would enjoy and be good at?

Of course, the most important thing will be for you to be Charlie; to be true to yourself. Be the kind of person whom I see in you now.

No matter what kind of job you have, what your job title is, how much or how little money the job pays, or what important or unimportant people say about your job, the most important thing about you will be **you.**

You are Charlie. That's what's most important. You are Charlie, and you happen to have this or that kind of job.

You will be older, have had more experiences, and will be wiser. You will have learned many new things.

Most importantly, I want you to be Charlie, whom I know and love—my friend.

What kind of a job will you have? What will you do with your interests and abilities?

The first thing to consider is that there are many jobs and places where you can apply your energies. You will know about some of them. There will be more that you haven't even thought of. So, find out about as many as you can. Check out the ones that sound like something you want to do and are able to do.

Many of us think that there are only a few jobs we can have, want to have, or have the ability to do. If we don't find one of these jobs, we throw up our hands and say, "There's nothing I can do!"

I used to think that. Then, one day, I met a man who was seventy-eight-years old. I liked him, and I could tell that he liked himself. I asked him what jobs he had had in his life. Do you know what he told me? He said, "I have had twenty-seven different jobs!" Wow! I figured out that there were so many different jobs to think about.

First, it's important to discover that there are many different jobs and things you can do in your life. Second, ask yourself, "What do I like, and what do I think I might be good at?" Charlie, what do you like? What do you think you might be good at? If you close your eyes and use your imagination, what do you imagine you want to be?

You might scratch your head and wonder about that. You could say, "I'm not sure." That's what most of us do, especially at your age. I suspect that would be true for you.

Begin to wonder some more about what you would like and are able to do. Write down what comes to your mind. Underline some things and say, "That could work." Other things you might mark through or erase and say, "No, I don't think so."

Future Horizons, Inc.

How about your autism? How does autism figure into what you might want to do?

Many autistic people are very good at concentrating on just a few things. They can learn more about these few things than people without autism can. Because of their autism, they can do much better at these few things than people without autism can.

People with autism often do well at math. They read well. They know computers. People with autism can really concentrate on these areas and do a good job.

On the other hand, people with autism don't do well in areas where they have to focus on different things at once. Because they get so concentrated on one thing, they don't notice other things around them.

For that reason, I don't think people with autism could play professional baseball. Why not? The answer is that there are so many things to concentrate on at one time. They might be looking in one direction and not be aware that someone is throwing the ball at them from another direction. Ouch! They might get hit in the head.

The same thing is true for being a race car driver, a pilot, or anything else where a person has to think about many different things at the same time. Also, because relating with other people is not something autistic people do easily, I wouldn't think they would be happy as a talk show host or a salesman.

However, people with autism might do very well where learning and using certain skills is more important than the ability to easily relate to other people. Taking into account your autism, as well as all the other parts of you, you will be the person to figure out what you want to do. You have to decide to change to something else, if that is what you want to do.

Sometimes, I think about different things you could do. I'll tell you what I have come up with so far, and as I watch you grow, I will tell you if I have any other ideas.

Because I think you are good with computers, I can see you doing something in the computer field. You related so well with your dogs and cats, you might want to do something with animals. Perhaps you could train seeing-eye dogs or companion dogs. You could work in the veterinary field or with the S.P.C.A..

Do you remember that I wrote earlier of Temple Grandin? I said I hoped you would read her books.

I think Dr. Grandin uses part of her autistic abilities to know cattle better than most people do. Because of that, she has a fine business making things better for cattle.

You could do the same thing with dogs or cats. You might use some of your abilities to know dogs or cats better than most people do. Because you could do that, you can help make things better for them.

I see your interest in the universe. Perhaps you would like work related to the stars and planets. You have an interest in recipes and cooking. Would you like to have a job in a restaurant or an ice cream store? I remember your saying, "Pots, I might grow up to be a scooper, an ice-cream scooper!"

Putting things in order means that you could be a file clerk, work in a warehouse, or be an employee of a medical supply store. You could also work in a library. Besides your ability to put things in order, you love books.

Do you remember Brother and Sister Bear in the library? Remember how important the library was to the mother with the baby, the elderly lady at the table, and the people checking books in and out?

Because you are good at math, you might work with numbers. You can repeatedly follow instructions, once you understand them, and you remember every detail. You could be an engineer or a repairman. You could repair air-conditioners, watches, generators, computers, and so many other interesting things.

You are so good with little children. You might have a job working with Mrs. Selby at Alief-Westwood Montessori School or work in another school.

I see how well you can memorize books and computer games, and how well you can say the words to them—with great feeling. You can look in the mirror and show all kinds of feelings. You might be an actor! Or, you might take that same ability and read stories to children. They would enjoy the way you make the stories come alive!

You play so well at Nintendo, are so good with the guidebooks and maps, and greatly enjoy the games, you might have a job creating new Nintendo games. Do you remember all the times we watched the "Cast of Characters" after you completed your games? Following the "Cast of Characters" would be the "Credits," the names of all the people who created the game. I remember saying, "Charlie, maybe one day your name will be there."

You have a beautiful singing voice, and I see how well you are doing with your piano lessons. Would you like to have a job in the music world? You seem to have a love for music, singing and dancing.

Looking at your Nintendo maps, writing them down and studying them, and then being able to get the message from your brain to your fingers is a real talent. I think you could do the same thing with music. Look at the music, learn to read it, and get the message from your brain to your fingers (or to your voice). Make the music you love!

Because you learn so well, are able to teach others (which you have done so many times with me), and are so good at learning new ways to say things, you might work for a book publisher. Perhaps because you have had to work so hard to use words, you say them with great appreciation and meaning. You could write books for children. You could also write books for people with autism.

If you become interested in the brain, you might work in a medical lab doing brain research. It seems to me that people who work in medical labs doing brain research need to be able to concentrate on a few things very well. They don't have to easily relate with others. And, when they do relate, it is usually in a quiet and factual way.

By the way, my neighbor is the chairman of a medical school department that does brain research. If you would like to know more about his work, I would be glad to ask him to show you his lab and tell you what the people in the lab do.

These are just a few of the jobs you might have! There are so many things you could do! You can do several things, not just one. Follow whatever interests you have and be open to developing new interests.

I once heard Gary Mesibov say that for some autistic children "work is play and play is work." I was reminded of what he said when I recently read an article about a man who gets paid for a job that he says is play for him. So, it may be that what is play for you might turn into valuable work.

You can have a job and then change to another job—and change again. You could have 27 different jobs, or you might have 72 different jobs!

You can pursue many of your interests without being paid for them. You can have many different interests at the same time, although one or two may be your main interests.

Follow your interests. Follow your dreams. Get help along the way. Let people whom you trust teach you, but make your own decisions.

You can think of this as an adventure, just as you play adventure Nintendo games. Go first through this game world, then the next, and the next.

Enjoy the journey, wherever it leads.

A few thoughts about being single or married

While you are thinking about what you want to do as an adult, you might wonder whether you want to remain single or be married.

I know a lot about being married. Nanny and I have been married for forty-four years. I have spent over thirty years helping people with their marriage problems.

What I discovered in all that time is that marriage is fine for some people, and being single is fine for other people. Being married is not something that everybody needs to do. Men and women can have great lives whether they are married or not.

As you think about whether you want to get married, I suggest that you talk it over with your mom and dad. They also know a lot about being married, and they know about being single. Plus, they know you!

You know that your parents will want you to make the right decision. They will want you to be happy with your choice to either get married or remain single. It's smart to talk with them before making your decision.

Whether you are married or single, you can have a good life! Married or single, you will have friends to talk with, listen to, share with, have fun with, teach and learn from.

Married or single; you will have friends whom you love, and friends who love you. You can have friends whom you care about and who care about you.
Being married can have many benefits, as those husbands and wives who are happily married can tell you. However,

Future Horizons, Inc.

being married can also present problems. Three of the problems that could be especially hard for someone with autism are as follows.

One of the biggest problems that married people have is socially interacting with each other. There are many social interactions between married people that are hard to understand and hard to do. There are numerous ways of socially interacting between a husband and wife that might be especially difficult for a man or woman with autism.

While social interaction is hard for many people, it is especially hard for people with autism. I think you may feel less pressure in social interactions if you are single.

Another big problem for married people is their strong expectations of each other. They are often not even aware of what some of these expectations are. Aware or not, a wife will expect her husband to be a certain way, and a husband will expect his wife to be a certain way. Each may want the other to change to fulfill the expectations. These expectations may be especially difficult for a person with autism to change to fulfill them.

Being single, your friends' expectations of you may not be as strong as your wife's expectations. Your friends may be better able to like and accept you as you are, not demanding that you change. And, you can like and accept your friends as they are, not demanding that they change.

A third problem in being married is about being together. I think that husbands and wives need to spend time together and time alone. But not every husband or wife sees it that way. In many marriages, a husband or wife has a hard time being happy when the other wants some time alone.

I think being single is easier to be alone when you want and to be with your friends when you want.

As you can see, there is much to think about when it comes to your choice to be married or single. Think about it, talk about it with your mom and dad, and decide what you think is best for you.

.hen people came to me to help them with their marriage problems, I asked them what they wanted their husband or wife to be. Often they would say, "I want him or her to always love me and be glad to see me."

I showed them a picture of a dog. I told them that dogs are very good at always loving us and being glad to see us, but men and women have a harder time doing that.

So, Charlie, whether you decide to be married or not, I think you should always have a dog (or a cat, if he or she is like Steve or Doug), who will always love you and be glad to see you.

Chapter Thirteen
God in Your Life

God loves me and is always with me.

Charlie, I include some thoughts about God. I started to leave this section out, but if I had, I wouldn't have told you about one of the most important things in my life. If I didn't say anything about how important God is, I would be leaving out something that is at the center of my life and could also make all the difference in your life.

I have never been able to prove that God exists, but at some point in my life, I chose to believe that He does exist.

Since that time, I have found an extraordinary source of strength and power, and most of all, love, in what I believe to be God. I believe that He loves me, cares about me, forgives me, and is always with me. I believe that God loves you, cares about you, forgives you, and is always with you. I believe that you can also find in Him an extraordinary source of strength, power, and love.

I know that you say your prayers every night. You, Andrew, mom, and dad say your prayers together. You thank God for everyone in your life and for all of His blessings. You ask for His love and guidance.

Therefore, you are praying to God now. Praying is another word for talking. I hope that you will never stop talking to God. If you do stop for a while, I hope that you will start talking to Him again.

One more thing. Do you remember that I wrote earlier that I try to spend the first hour or two of each day alone? Well,

I do. The most important part of that time is talking to God. I think that the most important part of the time Gandhi and Gautama spent alone each day was when they talked to God.

So, a suggestion: While you talk to God at bedtime, and any other time you want to, I hope that you will begin each day talking with Him. I think you will find this a big help.

Chapter Fourteen
Can You Help Yourself to Live the Life You Want to Live? Yes, You Can.

I can use my brain to help myself.

Discovering the life you want to live is something that takes most people years to figure out. I don't know what you will decide what you want for your life, but I can tell you that you can help yourself to live that life.

You probably won't have everything you want in your life, but none of us do. However, you may have more in your life than you can imagine. You can help yourself do that.

A blind person can use a seeing-eye dog or a white cane and can develop his or her sense of hearing. A blind person can learn to "read" books by feeling raised letters.

A hard-of-hearing or deaf person can wear hearing aids, use sign language, get a deaf-companion dog, or learn to read lips. A person who can't walk or for whom walking is very hard or very painful, can use a wheelchair, crutches, or canes to get around. This person can learn to use his or her arms to do some of the work the legs can't do.

All these people can decide that they are good people and that their disability (being blind, deaf or unable to walk) is not going to keep them from living their lives as best as they can.

Charlie, you can decide that, too. You can decide that you are a neat person and that being autistic is not going to stop you from living the life you want to live. You can decide that being autistic is not a curse, but a challenge. Living with autism is a challenge that you can wrestle with and come out as a winner.

Look back at Chapter One and later look at Chapter Fifteen when you think about having autism as a challenge. A challenge. is something that isn't easy. It takes work, but it is something you can do. You can be a winner!

We all have challenges, Charlie. Your challenge happens to be autism. Accept that you have autism. It is a part of you because of a few differences in your brain. However, autism is not all of you. There is so much more to you than having autism!

> *Charlie, you are a neat person.*
>
> *You can do so many things!*
>
> *You are an excellent reader.*
>
> *You are very good at math.*
>
> *You can concentrate on what you are doing.*
>
> *You have a remarkable sense of direction.*
>
> *You learn from what you see and then use what you have learned.*
>
> *You are a great Nintendo player.*
>
> *You can play the piano.*
>
> *You are honest, kind and caring.*

Future Horizons, Inc.

You work hard.

You are courageous.

I could go on and on about your skills and your qualities!

A girl who is blind can help herself with a seeing-eye dog, a white cane, and raised letters (for reading). A boy who is hard of hearing or deaf can help himself with wearing hearing aids, using sign language, and learning to read lips. A girl who can't walk, or for whom walking is very hard or painful, can help herself by using crutches or a wheelchair and developing the strength in her arms.

You can help yourself by learning and using certain skills that will help you in your relationships with other people. You may ask, "But, how, Pots; how can I do that?"

The way you can do that is by using other parts of your brain that enable you to learn relationship skills—skills that help you improve your relationships with other people. These are sometimes called social skills.

A "skill" is something you can do, like playing Nintendo, reading, or doing math. With another part of your brain, you can learn skills to help you with other people. You can learn to do what most people, whose brains are different from yours, seem able to do without having to use another part of their brains.

Charlie, do you remember the day Leo asked you why you came to the front door instead of the side door? One of the puppies had bitten you a month or so before, and you reminded Leo that the puppies were in the kitchen by the side door. So, you came to the front door. You told Leo, "I am a good thinker."

You were right. You were a good thinker then and a good thinker now. You have a good brain, a smart brain, and you can use it to help yourself.

Chapter Fifteen
Seeing Autism as a Challenge

I can accept the challenge of autism, and I can win.

Let's talk about seeing autism as a challenge. You have autism, and among the questions you need to ask are: "Is autism going to keep me from living a worthwhile and meaningful life, or is autism something that I can work with so that I can have that life?" "Does autism keep me from trying to live my life to the fullest, or can I live my life to the fullest anyway?"

That's the challenge: to live your life to the fullest with autism. I am convinced that this is a challenge you can accept and win!

Not long ago, after playing the three Donkey Kong Country games, you started to play Super Mario World. You hadn't played it in over a year, and so it was a challenge to play. You made some mistakes, but you corrected them.

You went on to beat all of the Resnors and Koopas! Following the Koopas came Bowser. You told me that you beat all of the Resnors and all of the Koopas, but that you could not beat Bowser.

After that, you confidently and happily went on to play Yoshi's Island. You felt good about beating the Resnors and the Koopas. Having tried to beat Bowzer a number of times and failing, you simply accepted that you could not beat him. You then went on to play another Nintendo game. What you showed me was that you had accepted the challenge of Nintendo, and you had won!

Charlie, Nintendo is a challenge. It is very hard for many people, and many of them will give up. They will say that they can't do it, and they will never play again.

It is also a challenge for you, and you have faced the challenge and won! That doesn't mean that you never make a mistake, and it doesn't mean that you have beaten every enemy. It **does** mean that you have developed into an excellent Nintendo player who can confidently and happily play the games.

The challenge didn't stop you and didn't beat you. Charlie, you learned all you could about the games, studied the maps, and practiced.

You are excited when you win, but you calmly accept that you can't always win. You know that you are an excellent player. You are a winner. In many ways, you have also accepted (and won) many of the challenges of autism.

By the way, do you know that some very famous people have faced challenges and gone on to win? Albert Einstein couldn't talk until he was four-years-old, and he couldn't read until he was nine-years-old. He then went on to become one of the world's greatest scientists.

Leonardo da Vinci, who had learning disabilities and often wrote backward, became a famous artist. Helen Keller was both blind and deaf but learned to read, write, and speak.

Thomas Edison wrote that he was a very poor student. He never learned grammar, and he couldn't spell. He went on to invent the light bulb, the phonograph, the microphone, and many other useful things.

George Patton couldn't read or write when he was twelve. Even in college, he needed a person to help him read. Later, Patton became one of the most famous generals of World War II.

The movie and television star, Christopher Reeve, after being paralyzed from falling from a horse, has gone on to act and direct movies. He can't walk or use his arms or hands, but he can still use his brain.

These people, and countless others not so famous, have faced their challenges and have won. Charlie, you are a winner when it comes to the challenge of Nintendo, and you are a winner when it comes to the challenge of autism.

Your autism caused you to stop talking when you were about two and a half-years. We didn't know if you would ever start talking again. With our help, and the help of other caring people, including speech therapists, you worked hard to start talking. You did it! By the time you were five, you were talking.

Before you talked, you might point to something you wanted. Then, one day, you said, "I want that." Before you talked, you would take my hand and pull me to the door. Then, one day, you said, "Pots, let's go."

You have accepted and won a challenge of autism.

For a long time, your autism caused you to insist that everything in your life be done exactly the same way every time. You got very upset if there were any changes. With help, you gradually allowed changes. You learned not to have things always the same all the time. You learned not to get so upset when things changed.

I remember when you insisted on going the same route from your house to Nanny's and my house. If I made one new turn, you would be unhappy. Now, you are no longer unhappy if I go a variety of routes. You might just say, "Pots, where are you going?"

You have accepted and won another challenge of autism.

For years, your autism caused you to think that you had to do everything perfectly. If you couldn't do something perfectly, you either became sad or refused to try. However, with help, you worked hard to win that challenge. After much work, you became very good at accepting that you can't do things perfectly!

For example, you had to win every battle Megaman fought with Dr. Wily and the other bad guys. So, you were sad much of the time you played the Megaman games. You now can play the Megaman games without having to always win. You can really enjoy the games. You don't have to always win to know that you are truly a winner.

Accepting what you can do and can't do makes you feel better. Sure, you're not perfect in accepting what you can't do, but that's the point; no one is perfect. However, you are clearly a winner at feeling good about what you can do and accepting what you can't do.

You have accepted and won another challenge of autism.

Autism makes it hard for you to know what to say in different situations. I think you have known that for years. I have seen you work on it. Many times you have asked me what you could say in different situations. You have asked what you could say to Andrew and Richard. You have told me what you could say if this or that happened.

I remember when you couldn't say anything in a situation, but I also remember the first time I heard you say something appropriate. You had fallen down our stairs. You got up, turned, looked at me, and said, "Barney doesn't cry." You had figured out that those words you had heard on a "Barney" videotape made sense to say when you fell down the stairs.

How very far you have come since that day. You say so many appropriate things in many different situations.

This is another challenge of autism that you have accepted and won.

Autism makes it hard for you to look another person in the eye; that is, to make eye contact. But, with help, you have worked hard to make eye contact.

Before, you would almost never look me in the eye. Now, you will look me in the eye, especially if you want to tell me something or see my reaction to something in which you are very interested. As we watch *Arthur's Reading Race* or *The Cat in the Hat*, you will turn and look me right in the eye!

You have accepted and won another challenge of autism.

Autism makes it hard for you to be aware of other people and their thoughts and feelings. With help, you have worked hard to be more aware of others and what they are thinking and feeling.

Some examples. You ask me what I am writing. You see a child who is sad, and you comfort the child. You tell your teacher, Mrs. Selby, that you are angry because she hurt your friend's feelings by making him go to the end of the line.

You have accepted and won yet another challenge of autism. The challenge of autism is to live your life to the fullest.

The challenge of your autism is really a series of challenges. As you can see, you have already accepted and won many of them!

Keep up the good work of accepting and winning the challenges of autism. Practice accepting and winning the challenges you have already won so that you won't forget how you won them. There will be more challenges of autism to come. When you recognize them, accept them and work on them with help. Continue to win!

Live your life to the fullest!

Chapter Sixteen
Twelve Skills You Can Use

Twelve things I can do to help myself.

Charlie, I'll now tell you about twelve skills that you can learn and use to help yourself. Some of these skills can help you in areas where that part of your brain that is autistic just doesn't automatically know things.

Some of the skills are just good life skills for all of us. Skill number five, "What you can do when you are cruelly teased," is a good life skill, and number twelve, "Look more at the good things in your life," is another one. I have included them with the skills to help you win the challenge of autism because I think they can be particularly useful.

I thought a long time before deciding on these twelve skills. I thought about what skills had helped me in my life and what skills had helped the people whom I had counseled over thirty years. Then, I thought about what skills would especially benefit people with autism.

While each person with autism is different, many people with autism have certain things that they are very good at, as well as other things that are very hard for them. I looked for skills that would help people with autism to better use the things they are good at, as well as help them do better in the things that may be hard for them.

People with high-functioning autism, which is what you have, have different needs than those with low-functioning autism. I thought about what skills would help you and others like you the most.

I asked myself, "What is hard and what is easy for you," Charlie; what skills would help you the most in your life?" While I am sure that other skills can be helpful for both you and other people with autism, I came up with the twelve skills that follow.

Just as you learn more about Nintendo and computer games, you learn skills to use in these games. In the same way, as you learn more about autism, I am sure that you can learn more skills to use in your life.

One last thing. When you add new skills to these twelve, be sure to write them down. Read them and read them again. Writing the skills down and reading and re-reading them will go a long way in helping you use them well.

Skill Number One: Taking Turns. *I talk and then I listen.*

Skill Number Two: I Could Say... When another person says something to me, I could say to him or her...

Skill Number Three: Look and Listen. *I look at, and listen to, people so I can know them.*

Skill Number Four: Smile. *I smile to myself and smile at others. This helps all of us feel better.*

Skill Number Five: What You Can Do When You Are Cruelly Teased. *What another person says or does to me will not keep me from knowing and liking myself.*

Skill Number Six: Write it Down—What you Can See. *I can learn so much from the visual image.*

Skill Number Seven: Practice—Repetition. *I learn by doing something over and over.*

Skill Number Eight: Plan, and Then Be Prepared to Change. *I plan ahead. I write it down. I read it and re-read it. I then decide that it will be all right if things change.*

Skill Number Nine: Organize. Organize. Organize. *I organize in detail because it helps me so much.*

Skill Number Ten: Organize To Do Something New. *I can organize to initiate something new. I can organize to create something new.*

Skill Number Eleven: Ask for help. *My asking for help is a very smart thing to do.*

Skill Number Twelve: Look More at the Good Things in Life. *I can be glad for the happy things and not be defeated by the sad things.*

Skill Number One
Taking Turns

I talk, and then I listen.

Because the autistic part of your brain doesn't automatically know how to talk with other people, you can help yourself by using other parts of your brain to learn how talking with another person works.

The first skill you can learn with another part of your brain is this: when you talk with another person, take turns. You share something about yourself, and then the other person shares something about himself or herself. Taking turns is the key—talking and then listening.

Sometimes, the time spent talking and listening is short. On other occasions, talking and listening produce longer conversations.

You can tell about your thoughts, what you like to do, or something that you think is interesting. You can listen while the other person does the same.

Taking turns talking and listening won't always work, but it will work enough of the time to use it as a guide. You may ask, "How do I know when it is time to talk? How do I know when it is time to listen?"

Here are some hints about when it is time to talk. When the other person asks you a question, it is your turn to answer his or her question. When the other person has stopped talking, and there is a silence, this usually means it is your turn to talk.

There are also hints about when it is time to listen. When you ask another person a question, it is time to listen to the answer. After you have talked for awhile, stop talking so that you can listen to the other person.

Start with these hints and practice taking turns talking and listening. As you get more practice, I think you will get a clearer idea of when to talk and when to listen.

By the way, in conversations with some people, you may have to do most of the talking. At other times, you may have to do most of the listening.

Not every person you meet will be very good at talking and listening, even if he or she is not autistic. Try not to be discouraged when what you do doesn't work.

Taking turns. It is a good way to talk with another person, so try to learn it and then practice it.

Skill Number Two
I Could Say...

When another person says something to me,
I could say to him or her...

The autistic part of your brain doesn't just automatically know what to say when you talk with other people. You can use another part of your brain to help you learn the skill of learning different things you can say when someone is talking to you. You decide which of these things seems most appropriate.

Learning this skill of what you could say will help you. I know you can do it. I've seen you do it many times.

You probably remember that you and I have recently worked on this skill. I asked, "What can you say when someone else says...?" You answered, "I could say..." We have talked about it many times, and we have used flashcards and fill-in-the blanks. Continue to do this, and develop and expand your learned choices of what you can say in different situations.

I have heard you say, "That was great, everyone. Thanks!" "I don't think so," or "No way " "Relax, Pots," "Are you impressed, Pots?"

When you arrived at our house one Thursday, I told you that I had to do several other things before we could play together. I had to feed the pups, check on a plumber working in our house, and make two telephone calls. You listened to me talk about everything else I had to do, and then you said, "What are you doing, Pots?"

I know that you had heard that phrase from one of the Berenstain Bears CD-ROMs. When Brother Bear and Sister Bear were yelling at each other, Papa Bear said to them, "What are you doing?"

I think you decided that you could say those words to me when I had so much going on at once. You made a good choice when you asked me, "What are you doing, Pots?"

A good choice, Charlie. Keep up the excellent work. I'm sure you will make good choices of what to say.

By the way, some very smart and successful people will often say, "I don't know what to say." And, sometimes, they might say, "I will think about it, and perhaps I can answer you later." You might use one of these answers.

You have already learned so many things you could say! I think you will have the adventure of learning many more, and I hope to have the joy of hearing you say some of them.

Skill Number Three
Look and Listen

I look at, and listen to, people so I can know them.

A third skill you can use to help yourself is another that will help you get along better with other people. Because the autistic part of your brain works in such a way as to make it hard to know another person, you can use another part of your brain to help you look at, and listen to, another person.

Just as I have already seen you use the "I could say" skill, I have also seen you use this skill. Several times I have watched you look at, and listen to, a child who is hurt or sad. You have gone over to comfort him or her.

You say something nice and then pat the child who was hurt or sad. You paid attention to what you saw and heard, and you decided that the child needed comfort. That's using the "look and listen" skill.

Because you have seen that I wear a hearing aid, and you have listened to me when I have told you that I don't hear very well, you have helped me hear you when I make mistakes about what you are saying to me. You will say to me, "Pots, look at me." And then you will say again what I was mistaken about. If I still don't understand what you said, you spell it for me.

You look at me, hear me, and then help me to understand what you are saying. That's also using the skill of looking at, and listening to, another person.

Charlie, do you see what you have accomplished? You made the effort to recognize when another child was hurt or

Future Horizons, Inc.

sad, and you appropriately comforted the child. You made the effort to recognize that I don't hear very well, and you appropriately asked me to look at you when you were speaking, and you even spelled the words for me.

These are two examples of using another part of your brain to observe and listen to another person, and then to respond appropriately.

Charlie, do you remember skill number one? Taking turns talking and listening. When the other person talks, he or she might tell you what he or she is interested in, thinking about, or perhaps likes to do.

Here is where this third skill comes in handy when you are talking with another person. It is just as important to listen as it is to talk. Plan on looking at the other person and listening to him or her.

When you listen, concentrate on **really** listening. Focus on what the other person is telling you. If you start thinking about something else, decide that you will think about that later, and then start listening again. This is really listening.

You can practice your listening at school, Cub Scouts, church, and home. Practice listening to your mom and dad. You can practice listening to me. Write down the names of the people with whom you could practice listening.

In addition to looking and listening, sometimes it is a good idea to ask about what you see or hear. If the person looks happy or sad, you could ask, "Are you happy?", or, "Are you sad?"

If the person is telling you something, ask questions about what he or she is saying. You could say, "That's interesting. Please tell me more."

Sometimes, you can just ask, "How do you feel?" or, "What are you thinking?". The person may be glad you asked, because it means you care enough about him or her to ask. Most of the time, the other person will be glad you used this skill, and you will be glad, too.

Future Horizons, Inc.

Skill Number Four
Smile

*I smile to myself and smile at others, and this
helps all of us feel better.*

A fourth skill that you use to help yourself is to smile.
That's it—smile!

Nothing is too hard about smiling. In fact, I am told that it
takes fewer facial muscles to smile than to frown.

Smiling is not difficult, but most of us don't do it enough.
When smiling doesn't come naturally, we do it because we
have learned to do it.

I even remember a song about smiling. When I was a boy,
we used to sing a song that had the words, "Pack up your
troubles in your old kit bag, and smile, smile, smile!"

Why smile? How can you help yourself by smiling?

First, I think smiling can help you feel better, more at ease,
and less frightened. It can help you see things in a nicer
and more positive way. Smiling can help you be more open
to others. Second, I think your smiling can come across to
others as being friendly, caring and kind. Most people like
that. They appreciate your smiling at them. It helps them
feel better.

I will always remember a young woman who worked at the
reception desk at the rehabilitation hospital in the Medical
Center. She was badly crippled and had all sorts of
stainless steel braces on both her arms and her legs.

I was amazed, with all that was crippled about her body, she had the courage and will to do a job where she had to help people. But what I remember most about her was her smile. With all that she had to struggle with, she still always gave me a big smile. I admired her for that smile. I found that I began to smile more, all because of her and her smile.

I am not saying that you should smile all of the time. There are times when it would really seem strange to smile; times when you wouldn't want to smile. You wouldn't smile when you are sad or someone else is sad. I think the best thing I can say is to smile if it seems to you like it might be a good time to smile.

Charlie, I think that you have a great smile. Just as you use the mirrors in our playroom to practice all kinds of looks, practice smiling into the mirror and see for yourself how it looks. I think you will like what you see.

Smiling is something all of us would do well to do more of. It is a helpful skill for you and a help to others around you.

Skill Number Five
What You Can Do When You Are
Cruelly Teased

*What another person says or does to me will not
keep me from knowing and liking myself.*

Another skill you can use to help yourself is to learn what
you can do when people are mean to you. There are things
to do when you are put down or when others say mean
things that hurt your feelings. Learning what to do when
others make fun of you is very important.

There is kind teasing, and there is cruel teasing. Kind
teasing doesn't make us feel bad. It can be done by people
who really like us and don't want to hurt our feelings. You
tease me sometimes, and we both laugh and enjoy it.

People using cruel teasing are trying to make us feel bad,
and it is a bad thing to do to anyone. All of us are cruelly
teased for one thing or another, and we try to figure out
what to do when it happens.

For you, I imagine that most of the time you will be cruelly
teased about being autistic. This is because most people
don't understand autism, and all they see is that you are
different from them. Some of them will try to put you
down about it. It's a bad thing to cruelly tease you, or to
cruelly tease anyone, but some people will do it anyway.

So what do you do when this happens? First, you need to
know that when some person cruelly teases you, it shows
that the person has a problem. You need to know that it
doesn't mean that there is anything wrong with you.

What is wrong is that the other person is doing something cruel. He or she tries to make it look like something is bad about you, but the truth is that the cruel teasing shows that there is something wrong with that person.

Second, you need to know that you, and you alone, can decide the kind of person you are. You won't let someone else decide that.

Other people can say whatever mean things they want about you, but you decide that what they say is not going to change how you see yourself. It is not going to change how you think or feel about yourself.

What kind of person are you? You will be the best one to answer that question. Don't accept what the cruel teaser says about you. Instead, look in the mirror and ask what you say about yourself.

I have watched you carefully for eleven years. I have spent a lot of time with you, and I have gotten to know you very well. Based on that experience, and being very honest with you, I can tell you what kind of person I think you are.

I think that you are a fine and wonderful person.

I respect and admire you.

You are kind.

You are courageous.

You are fair.

You are a good friend.

You are my best friend.

You are also smart; you are intelligent.

You want to learn new things.

You do your best.

Just think of all the things you can do! You can do so many things and do them well, even with having autism. You do more and show more courage and intelligence than most people who don't have autism.

Here is a true story I want to share with you. Several years ago, there was a major league baseball player who was thought to be one of the best first basemen ever. One day during a World Series game, he made a mistake. He allowed a ground ball to roll between his legs.

Because of that one mistake, this player was cruelly teased by thousands of people. He was booed then and for years afterward—all for just one mistake.

This hurt the player a lot, but he finally figured out what to do when people put him down. His name is Bill Buckner. He played for the Boston Red Sox, and this is what he finally decided about himself: "All I have to do is live with myself. I have to like myself."

He had come to like himself, so although others could cruelly tease him, they couldn't make him not like himself. They could try to put him down, but he wouldn't let them get him down.

Charlie, that's what you can do—like yourself. There is so much to like! No matter how hard people try to put you down, you won't let them get you down.

That's what's most important: knowing and liking yourself. Then, when someone makes fun of you, what he or she says won't keep you from liking yourself.

I will give you a few other tips on what to do when someone cruelly teases you. Sometimes, you can ignore it. Don't look at the person and don't answer him or her.

Often, you can say something that I and a lot of other people being cruelly teased used to say, "Sticks and stones may break my bones, but names will never hurt me."

Sometimes, you can laugh it off. What does it mean, "to laugh it off?" This means that you have decided that you like yourself, no matter what mean thing someone says about you. And, because you like yourself, you can see that what the person is saying mean about you just isn't true.

So, you can laugh to yourself because you like yourself, and the cruel teaser is wrong. The person saying the mean thing may want you to cry, but you can laugh instead.

If someone tries to make you feel bad by saying something mean about your autism, you can ask that person, "Do you just want to make me feel bad, or would you really like to know about autism?" Then you can say, "I'll tell you about my autism, if you really want to know." (Please read again the last section of Chapter Seven before you try to tell someone else about your autism.)

Future Horizons, Inc.

For example, if someone says something cruel about your brain, ask that person if he or she would like you to describe what your brain is really like. You can tell the person that your brain is like his or hers in most ways, but it is different in some ways.

If a person says that you "just don't get it" when it comes to something he or she has said, you can ask if you could describe what autism really is. Perhaps that person will then understand and appreciate why it is so hard for you to "get it," and how much effort you make.

Some people who try to put you down are just jerks, and they won't care about really knowing you. It's better that you see them for the jerks they are and not spend your time telling them about you.

However, some people who put you down are not jerks; they have just done a really stupid thing by making fun of you. When you give them the chance to really know you, they become ashamed of cruelly teasing you and begin to like and admire you.

Skill Number Six:
Write it Down—What You Can See

I can learn so much from the visual image.

Here is a sixth skill that you can use to help yourself. It is a skill that will help you understand things better.

Because the autistic part of your brain works in such a way as to make it hard to understand and respond to what you hear, you can use another part of your brain to understand and respond to what you **see**. When you understand something that you can see, you also can better understand what you hear.

A lot of autistic people do much better with what they see rather than with what they hear. As I have watched you over the years, I am sure this is true for you, too.

There have been so many times when I have talked with you about something, and you have just not responded to what I said. So, I would write it down, you would read it, and then you would respond! You got it! You understood!

I remember when you were in kindergarten at River Oaks Montessori School, and you had a teacher named Mr. Doug. You liked him a lot. He liked you a lot. I remember your taking a pad and pencil to Mr. Doug when you wanted to understand what he had said. He would write it down, and when you read it, you understood what he had said. Charlie, you were just five-years-old when you did that.

Long before you learned to read, I remember your watching parts of "Sesame Street." You could see what was on the television screen, and you learned so much from what you

Future Horizons, Inc.

saw. You would watch the same parts over again, as if you wanted to soak up what you could see with your eyes.

As you know, I think that you are the best Nintendo player I have ever seen. I think that one of the several reasons that that you are is that you look at the maps in the guidebooks, understand what you see on the maps, and then use what you have seen when you play the games.

By the way, I said earlier that I hoped you might some day read books on autism by Temple Grandin. I have never met her, but I have read her books, and I know people who know her. You might start with one book in particular, *Thinking in Pictures*. Dr. Grandin talks about learning from what you see. I am very curious to know whether you think in the same ways as she does—"in pictures." Check it out for yourself. See what applies to you and what doesn't apply to you.

You also might be interested in one thing Temple Grandin wrote about an autistic woman named Donna Williams. Donna Williams is very well known and has written books on autism.

Dr. Grandin writes of Donna Williams, *"Like me, she had to see every step written on paper. If the smallest step is left out, the autistic mind will be stumped. The visual image of the written steps is essential."*

Charlie, I put the above statement in italics because I think that it is so important. I keep it framed on my desk, and I read it every day. Temple Grandin says that it is true for her, as well as for Donna Williams. Charlie, I think it is true for you, too.

While we are on the subjects of writing things down and the importance of what you can see, did you know that television anchor men and women are reading the news that they broadcast on their news programs? As we watch them, it appears that they are looking right at us, right into the lens of the camera. Much of the time, however, they are looking right next to the camera lens at written words we don't know are there. And, have you ever noticed that they look down from time-to-time? That's because they also have a written script in front of them.

When many people, including the President of the United States, give a speech, they write down what they want to say, study what they have written, and then, while they are giving their speech, they look at the words on something called a teleprompter. How important writing it down is to them! How important what they can see is to them!

I hope that you will take this skill, which you already have, and develop it more. Pay attention to what you can see, whether it is in pictures or words.

I believe that you will find this skill well worth using!

Skill Number Seven
Practice—Repetition

I learn by doing something over and over.

A seventh skill you can use to help yourself is to repeatedly practice what you are trying to understand or do.

The important words here are "practice" and "repetition," to repeat what you are trying to understand or do. The more you repeat, the more you practice, the more successful you will be.

Again, I think this is something that you already know is true for you. You already know it, and so I am saying that you are right!

I have seen you use repetition and practice so many times. As I said earlier, even when you were just a few-years old and would watch "Sesame Street" in your highchair, you would want to see the same parts repeated. Over-and-over you would say, "Rewind!"

I used to worry that you repeated too much. I worried that you, like many other autistic children, would just keep on repeating the same thing. I realize now that you knew better than I did about the great value in repeating. The value was that by using repetition, you learned.

That was it, you learned. By repeating things, you made what you saw a part of you, so that you could understand and use that knowledge later.

Even now, when you play Nintendo games, I see you repeating different parts of the game. You will read and re-

read the guidebook maps and play and re-play the games. You are an excellent Nintendo player.

I also see you watching the same computer CD-ROMs over and over. You then can recite every word of them. Not only can you say all of the words, but you also say them with meaning and feeling.

I have enjoyed listening to your reciting *Tortoise and the Hare*, by Aesop, *Arthur's Reading Race*, by Marc Brown, and *Sheila Rae the Brave*, by Kevin Henkes. I have really enjoyed your telling me these stories, as well as many others. By repeatedly watching them and learning each word and feeling, you have become a very good storyteller. This is a wonderful thing.

You can practice what you are trying to do or understand with me, just as you are doing now. Practice with your mom and dad and other family members and close friends. Your teachers are there to help you with practice.

Even your cats can help, even though they don't speak words. You can practice in front of a mirror, just as you do now in our playroom.

Repetition.

Practice, practice, practice.

Repetition and practice.

It works for you.

Skill Number Eight
Plan and Then Be Prepared to Change

I plan ahead and write it down. I read and re-read. I decide that it will be all right if things change.

An eighth skill you can use to help yourself is to plan and then be prepared to change.

Experts say that autistic people have trouble dealing with change. The truth is that almost all people have trouble with change, but it is just harder for autistic people. You do much, much better at change than you used to do.

I remember, when you were much younger, you would get terribly upset if we even went one block out of our usual drive from your house to our house.

You wanted everything to be done the same way as it had been done before. No changes! You have improved so much since then!

One example that comes to mind is when we have to change the days you are coming to our house. It used to be that you would get very upset if we had to change the days. Now you just take it in stride and accept it. You will say, "If I can't come today, I will come another day."

To use this skill is to plan each day and each thing you are going to do ahead of time. Think about the next day and about each thing you are going to do, before you actually start doing it. Write it down and look at what you have written. Then, and only then, do it.

Once I have planned my day or something I am going to do that day, and have written it down on paper, I feel much more prepared and at ease.

I started getting up before five o'clock in the morning when your mother was a little girl, just to have an hour or two to prepare before everyone else got up. During part of that time, I planned my day. Then I would write it down. Doing that helped me to be less anxious, and I felt more in control of myself and my day.

I have also found that once I have planned ahead and put the plan on paper, I am better able to handle changes. Sometimes, after I have written down what's going to happen that day, I then write, "Some of this will change, and that will be all right."

If you are going to call someone on the telephone, write down a few words of what you want to say before you call. If you are going to meet with someone, you could write on paper what you want to say at the meeting.

Actors in movies, television, and plays rehearse before their performances. They read a written script of what they are going to say. They practice saying the words over-and-over before they actually say the words in the movie, television show or play.

It works for them. It can work for you.

Plan ahead. Write it down. Read and re-read.

Then decide that it will be all right if things change.

Future Horizons, Inc.

Skill Number Nine
Organize. Organize. Organize.

I organize, in detail, because it helps me so much.

Charlie, I have already written about organizing different things in your life in skills sections number six, seven and eight. You might want to read about these skills again.

I call this section on skill number nine, "Organize. Organize. Organize." I repeat the word "organize" three times because it is so important.

In this section, I talk about some examples of how you have already organized things in your life. I then describe some skills you can use to organize now and in the future.

I think most people with autism have trouble organizing things, and I think that also might be true for you. So what can you do about getting organized? The answer is that you can learn to organize. You can do it.

Can you learn to organize? Yes, you can..

Why do I think you can do this? I have seen you organize. That's why I know that you can do it.

Like so many children with autism, from the time you were very young, you would line up all kinds of different things. They were always in the same order and in the same way. You would line up blocks and train cars. Your plastic alphabet letters were always in alphabetical order. You lined them up and organized them.

You learned how to read your Nintendo maps. You saw how they were organized, and you used that organization when you played your games. You took what you read and organized it to help you win the challenge of Nintendo.

With help from your mom and dad, your teachers, and me, you learned to follow a sequence—to put things in order, do one thing first, and then do the next thing. You learned to put work to be done on the left and work you had already done on the right. Remember the "start tray" on the left and the "finish tray" on the right of our desk? When you knew how to follow a sequence, you were organizing.

You saw, with our help, what to do first each day, what to do following that, and what to do next. You learned to organize your day from the first to the last task.

At first, we wrote down what you were going to do each day. You read it, understood it, and were able to do it. Now, we often only write things down when you are going to do something different.

You learned to look at a calendar to see what was planned for the coming days. That's organizing.

By the way, many of the organizational skills that you learned were from some of the many ideas we got from Gary Mesibov and Division TEACCH. As I wrote elsewhere, you can ask Gary Mesibov and his friends at Division TEACCH for help. You can ask him and them for help with more ideas on how to organize.

You read the instructions on how to be line leader at your school, and you were able to organize yourself to be an excellent line leader.

What skills do you need to organize now and in the future? Here are skills you can use.

First, think about what you want to organize.

Second, ask for help in how to organize it.

Third, write down, in detail, what you need to do to organize it.

Fourth, read what you have written down.

Fifth, read it several times.

Sixth, practice it repeatedly

I want to say something about the second skill you just read, "Second, Ask for help in how to organize it."

Charlie, autism makes you very good at following organizational systems (the ways things are organized) if someone else sets the systems up and shows you how to use them. Autism makes it difficult for you to set up your own systems, and autism can cause you to take longer to understand the way someone else has organized things.

However, once you understand the organizational system someone developed for you, and you understand the way the person has organized it, your autism helps you to do a great job of following that organizational system. In fact, if you look at the examples I have given at the beginning of this section, you can see that you are clearly a winner at following organizational systems!

Think about these six skills you can use now and in the future. Think about what you want to organize. Ask for help. Write down in detail what you need to do to organize things. Read what you have written down. Read it again and again. Practice it over and over.

These are not the only skills you can use to organize. You can add other organizational skills to them, and I hope that you will. In the meantime, these can be useful skills.

Future Horizons, Inc.

Skill Number Ten
Organize To Do Something New

*Here is a way I can initiate something new.
I can create something new.*

I want to talk to you about how your organizational skills can help you do new things; and how you can use these skills to create or initiate new things.

Many people with autism have a difficult time doing new things. It is hard for them to initiate and create something new.

People with autism tend to do the same things over and over, in the same way, and have trouble when it comes to doing something different. I think that may also be true for you, Charlie. So, what do you do?

While there are different ways to do new things, create, and initiate, I think the best answer for you is to learn to organize to do new things. I think that this is a smart way for you learn how to create and initiate new things.

Can you use this way to do new things? Can you learn to create and initiate new things? Yes, I think you can. I'll tell you why.

I have seen you do new things. I have seen you initiate and create something new.

When you were ready, you took some of your lined-up blocks and made different buildings with them. You took some of your lined-up train cars and made trains with them.

You made different kinds of trains. This was initiating and creating something new.

With your plastic letters, you spelled words, such as "dog" and "cat." Then you made up words. You created new words that no one else used. You initiated new words and tried to pronounce them. You smiled when you did that! You made something new. You created and initiated something new.

You love the *Living Books* CD-ROMs. You enjoy playing them and have memorized them.

Using the cursor on the computer and highlighting the words in out-of-order ways is fun for you. You make nonsensical sentences from them and laugh when you say, "That doesn't make any sense!" Charlie, that is doing something new. It is initiating. It is creating.

Also, you like to stand in front of the mirror and imitate the characters in the *Living Books*. When you tell me the stories you have memorized, with great feeling and even sound effects, you are doing something new and creative.

When you draw the computer screen sticker pictures, write the words that describe them on paper, and make a matching game with them, this is initiating something new.

Now that you can see that you can do new things, create, and initiate, what skills do you need to do that now and in the future? Here are skills you can use.

- First, decide that you want to do something new. Decide that you want to create and initiate new things.

- Second, listen to any ideas, thoughts, or dreams you may have that are new. Write them down and think about them.
- Third, make a list of new things you might want to do. Select one thing from your list. Write it down.
- Fourth, spend time thinking about what you have decided to do. What do you know about it, and what do you need to learn?
- Fifth, write down all of what you know about the thing you want to do.
- Sixth, get help learning how to do that new thing. Ask others. Do research.
- Seventh, write down the new things you have learned from others and from your research.
- Eighth, organize what you have written down. Organize what comes first, second, third, etc.
- Ninth, always think, write, think again, and write again. Get more help along the way. Do that until you think you have it about right.—not until it is perfect, because it is not going to be perfect.
- Tenth, take a deep breath. Relax. Be calm. Then do your something new! Create it! Initiate it!

Charlie, you have been creating, initiating, and doing something new during all of these ten steps. Congratulations. You have run the race and crossed the finish line. Enjoy doing something new!

Here are two examples of following these skills. The first example is how your mom and dad went about creating the plan for the new playroom for your house.

First, they decided to do something new. Your parents wanted to initiate and create something.

Second, they listened to any ideas, thoughts, or dreams they may have had that were new. They wrote them down, and they thought about them.

Third, your parents made a list of new things they might want to do, and they selected one thing from their list. They selected adding a new playroom to your house. They wrote this down.

Fourth, your mom and dad spent time thinking about what they had decided to do. They asked, "What do we know about adding a new playroom to our house?" They then asked, "What do we need to learn about adding a new playroom to our house?"

Fifth, your parents wrote down all they knew about adding a new playroom to your house.

Sixth, your mom and dad got help for what they needed to learn to add that playroom. They asked others and did research. They asked an architect to tell them what they needed to know. They asked him to draw on paper what their new playroom might look like. They asked him to make a list of things needed for the new playroom.

Seventh, they wrote down what they had learned from others. They wrote down what they had learned from the architect and what they had learned from their research.

Eighth, your parents organized what they had written down. They organized what would come first, second, third and all the way to the end.

Ninth, your mom and dad thought, they wrote more, they thought again, and wrote again. They received more help along the way. They talked to the architect several times. They talked to Mr. Bumpass, the builder, and they talked to him again. They made changes, and more changes. They did that until they thought they had it about right. It didn't have to be perfect (they knew it could never be perfect). They just kept thinking, getting help, and writing down about adding the new playroom until they thought they had it about right.

Tenth, your mom and dad took a deep breath. They relaxed. They calmed down. Then they told Mr. Bumpass to build the new playroom. They told him how they wanted it to be, just the way they had decided it would be. They had created the plan of your new playroom! They had initiated the building of the new playroom as they had created it to be!

The second example is how I organized to do something new. It is how I went about writing this guidebook for your living with autism.

First, I decided that I wanted to do something new. I wanted to initiate and create something.

Second, I listened to any ideas, thoughts, or dreams I may have had that were new. I wrote them down and thought about them.

Third, I made a list of new things I might want to do. I selected one thing from my list. I selected writing a guidebook for your living with autism. I had looked for such a guidebook, but couldn't find one. I wasn't sure that I could write one, but I felt it was very important for you to have a guidebook for your autism. I decided that would be the new thing I would do. I wrote it down.

Fourth, I spent time thinking about what I had decided to do. I asked, "What do I know about autism?" Then I asked, "What do I know about Charlie?" And I asked, "What skills have I learned in my own life, and in my job of counseling people about their lives, that might be especially helpful to Charlie? What could I write in a guidebook for Charlie to use as he lives with autism? What do I need to learn?"

Fifth, I wrote all I knew about autism and you. I listed all the skills that had helped me live my life and had helped the people whom I had counseled. As I wrote it all down, I began thinking of how I could make a guidebook from what I had written. With that in mind, I kept writing about autism and you. I kept writing about what would be needed in a guidebook.

Sixth, I got help for what I needed to learn. I did research. I knew you well. I was familiar with the skills that had helped me in my life and the skills that helped the people whom I had counseled about their lives. I had read much about autism and had listened to others who knew about autism. I decided that I needed to read more and learn more about autism. So I read more and thought more.

Seventh, I wrote down the new things I had learned about autism from others and from my research.

Always write it down. Put it on paper so you can see it and read it.

Eighth, I organized what I had written. I decided what came first, second, third, fourth etc. I also did the same for the guidebook.

Future Horizons, Inc.

Ninth, I thought more and wrote more. I thought again and wrote again. I changed things by removing or adding things. I changed the words so many times!

At long last I had written all I could think of and had come to the end of writing my thoughts. However, I still didn't think that I had the guidebook about right. I wanted to show it to others whom I respected and whose opinions I valued. I wanted their thoughts and suggestions of how to make it better.

I asked your mom and dad to read the guidebook and tell me what changes they thought I should make so that it would be a better book. I asked Gary Mesibov to read it, and to tell me what changes he thought I should make so that it would be a better guidebook.

Your mom and dad and Gary Mesibov told me what they thought about how to make this a better guidebook. They suggested things to add and things to leave out. They gave me good reasons for their suggestions. They had some really good ideas, and I was so glad they spent so much time reading what I had written and sharing their thoughts with me.

When I felt that the guidebook was about right, and your mom and dad (and Gary Mesibov) thought it was about right, I was ready for the tenth step. I knew that I was ready to finish it.

The tenth step: I took a deep breath. I relaxed and became calm. I read the guidebook one more time. I thought about it again. I made some small changes. I was really finished!

I had done something new. I had created and initiated it. The ten steps to do something new were now done. Here was a guidebook for you to use as you live with autism.

These are just two examples of how to organize to create or initiate something new. Maybe they can help you.

Charlie, you can do these ten steps. You have the ability to do them. You can organize to create and initiate so many new things. I have seen you do it!

There is something else to remember. You read about it in Chapter Ten. That was the chapter entitled, "Mistakes."

Everyone makes mistakes. It just happens to all of us.

Your mom and dad made mistakes when they organized to add the new playroom to your house. Their architect made mistakes. Mr. Bumpass, the builder, and his workmen made mistakes. But, with help, they discovered their mistakes and learned from them. They discovered the mistakes, learned from them, and corrected them.

I made mistakes when I organized to write your guidebook. With help, I discovered them, corrected them, and learned from them. That's what you can do when you make mistakes in organizing something new. Like your parents and me, you can discover the mistakes, learn from them and then correct them.

Why should you organize to create, initiate, and do something new? I think it can be exciting for you—an adventure. You can learn something. Enjoy!

Future Horizons, Inc.

Skill Number Eleven
Ask for Help

Asking for help is a very smart thing to do.

An eleventh skill to help yourself is to ask for help from other people.

You are good at asking for help. You are also are very good at thanking someone who helps you.

I am glad that you ask for help and are thoughtful enough to thank the person who helps you.

You can ask for help from family, friends, classmates and teachers. You can ask Gary Mesibov and Kaia Mates for help. Your mom can tell you about them and introduce you to them. They know a lot about autism, and they know you.

Ask your friends and classmates to help you. Let them know to tell you if you are not paying attention to them when they are talking to you.

Say to them that being autistic means that you can easily become distracted by something in your mind and forget that they are with you and are trying to talk to you.

Your friends should know that you like them, and you want to listen when they are talking to you. Tell them you appreciate being reminded, in a nice way, that you are not paying attention.

I try to always stand up straight. I want to stand up straight. But there are times when I slump over and don't realize it.

If I am with your mother or Nanny, one will say, "You're doing it again. You're slumping over. Stand up straight." I will thank them for reminding me.

Sometimes, when I am concentrating on something someone is telling me, I scowl. When I scowl I look like I am mad when I'm really not mad. So Nanny will say to me, "You're scowling." I will stop scowling. I will thank Nanny for reminding me.

When you are playing a Nintendo game, I sometimes close my eyes and fall asleep. I will hear you say, "Wake up, Pots!" I thank you for waking me up, because I don't want to fall asleep while I watch you play a Nintendo game.

You can invite your friends and classmates to say, "Charlie, you're doing it again. You're not paying attention to us." You can thank them, because you **do** want to pay attention when they are talking to you.

Also, if you find that you didn't hear something being said or missed something being done, because you were thinking about something else, ask for help. Tell those around you that your mind had wandered and ask for help for what you missed.

You might smile, and say, "Whoops. There I go again. I was concentrating on something in my mind. Please tell me what I missed."

Asking for help is a very smart thing to do.

Future Horizons, Inc.

Skill Number Twelve
Look at the Good Things
in Your Life

*I can be glad for the happy things and not be
defeated by the sad things.*

A twelfth skill you can use to help yourself is to look more
at the good things in your life.

Is looking more at the good things in your life a skill? Is it
something you can learn? Yes, it is a skill and can be
learned. Most importantly, you can learn it.

Learning this skill means that you first learn that you have a
choice of how you look at your life. You can choose to
look at your life as a good life or a bad life. You can
choose to look more at your blessings, on the good things in
your life. On the other hand, you can choose to look more
at your hurts, the sad things in your life

To look more at the good things in their lives is a choice
that just seems to come easy to some people, but for a lot of
people, who have had hurts and sadness in their lives, it's a
hard choice to make.

For some people, who suffer from depression, it is a choice
that seems almost impossible. Yet, even for them, there
can be help for their depression and help to look at the good
things in their lives.

Looking more at the good things in your life means to look
on the bright side of things, not the dark side.

It is for you to be glad that you are you and not sad that you are you. It is looking at what you can do, rather than looking at what you can't do.

Someone once said that to look more at the good things is like looking at a glass and seeing it half-full, rather than seeing it half-empty. Another person said that to look more at the good things is like taking a lemon, which is sour, and adding sugar and water to make lemonade, which is sweet.

According to another wise person, it is better to spend our time being thankful for our blessings rather than being sad about our hurts. Someone else said that it is better to spend more time thinking about our abilities rather than thinking about our disabilities.

I think that you have so many good things in your life. You can do many things and do them well!

You can see, hear, and use your arms and legs!

You are great at Nintendo and reading and math!

You can learn all of the words of entire stories, and repeat them outloud with appropriate meaning!

You can play the piano!

You are a wonderful son!

You are a wonderful grandson!

You are a wonderful student!

You are a wonderful friend!

Your mom and dad love you so much! Your brothers, Andrew and Max, and your sister, Whitney, love you. You are loved by so many.

If some of us are not here when you read this, always know that we love you! Whether we've moved away, or gone to be with God in Heaven, we will always love you. And you have given, and give us now, so much love!

Choosing to look at the good things in your life makes it easier to smile than to frown. Looking at the good things makes you friendlier to others. Looking at the good things in your life makes it easier not to be bitter, not to always think of yourself as a victim.

Yes, you have autism. You live in a world where most people don't understand autism. But some of them would like to understand, so try to find them and teach them. Teach them about you, and you learn about them.

For those who don't want to understand, you can say, "So long, Adios." You can go on and live your life with those people who **do** want to know you and want you to know them. At times, that will be tough. So, what do you do? The answer is that you toughen up!

If someone doesn't accept you and like you, then you choose to accept and like yourself! You choose to be in the company of people who do accept you and want to be with you! If someone puts you down, then pick yourself up! When someone says something to make you feel bad, then choose to look at the wonderful things in your life so that you can feel good!

Choosing to look at the good things in your life means that you can hold your head high and face whatever comes. It means that you can be glad for the happy things and not be defeated by the sad things.

To look more at the good things in your life is a choice that you make. It is a choice that you make every day.

The above are twelve skills to start with that will help you. Some of these skills will help you in those areas where that part of your brain that is autistic doesn't just automatically know something. Some of these skills are just good life skills.

Charlie, I invite you to try these twelve skills. It's O.K. if you make mistakes. It's O.K. if you fail. Just dust yourself off and try again.

Future Horizons, Inc.

Chapter Seventeen
My Affirmation

I am Charlie.

I like myself.

I am glad that I am me.

Charlie, an affirmation is a statement that something is true. When you make an affirmation, you say that something is true and correct.

I think that it is very important that each of us say an affirmation about ourselves. I know that is true for me. I believe that it is true for you.

Many people probably don't say an affirmation about themselves. They probably don't think about it. The problem with not thinking about it is that people may not have a very good idea about their identity. They could think some bad things about themselves that are not true.

I don't want you to not have a very good idea of your identity. I don't want you to end up thinking some bad things about yourself that are not true.

I do want you to know who you are. I want you to know what is true.

I hope that you have found in what I have written some clearer idea of whom you are. I haven't written everything about you. Only you can finally know the person you are.

Think about what you have read here. Add it to your own thoughts, and think some more. Write it down and then do something for fun. Play with your pets, play Nintendo, or think about something else. Do whatever you want to do.

From time-to-time, think about what you have read here. Think more about yourself. Ask, "What is true about me?"

Write an affirmation of what you think is true and correct about you. Make it as simple and brief as possible and make it positive. Then say it. Repeat it every day. Sometimes, say it many times in a day.

That way you make it a part of you. You can say your affirmation to a good friend, but you don't have to. I hope you will say it to someone who loves you, so that he or she can affirm back to you that you are right.

As a place to start, you might use what I have written on the next page. It is an affirmation of you as I see you.

My Affirmation

I am Charlie.

I love. I am kind. I am fair. I care.

I am honest. I have courage.

I am intelligent. I am sane.

I can do many things.

I do my best.

I have autism.

*I do my best to accept and win the challenge
of autism to live my life to the fullest.*

I like myself.

I am glad that I am me.

A shortened, and easier to remember affirmation, which
you could say many times, could be:

My Affirmation

I am Charlie.

I like myself.

I am glad that I am me.

You can have two affirmations: a long one and a shorter one. Both will help you.

Future Horizons, Inc.

Chapter Eighteen
Last of All

I think I can.

Well, Charlie, I have written a lot for you to think about. I suggest that you think about only part of it at a time. Read and think about part of it now. Read and think about another part later.

You have so much to be happy about. I hope that you spend time thinking about that, and I hope that you enjoy all that you have to be glad about.

You are a wonderful boy! I believe that you will be a fine man! Your courage, kindness, and honesty have changed our lives so much for the better. Just being you has brought us joy. We are proud and thankful to call you our friend.

Being with you has been like opening a window and letting in the fresh air and sunshine.

You are Charlie!

Your autism is just a small part of you.

You are so much more than your autism.

I hope that you will put to good use the best parts of having autism. In addition, I hope that you will use other parts of your brain to learn skills that don't come automatically to you because of autism.

Autism is a challenge. I hope that you will accept the challenge and be the winner I know you to be.

Charlie, I have written so much you can do to help yourself. I am sure that you can find even more ways to.

You may say, "This is too much to do!" You may say, "I can't do all of this!" I understand how you might feel this way, but I believe that you can do all of this, and more!

I remember when you were playing "Yoshi's Island." You were about to fight Naval Piranha. I always thought he was the toughest one to beat, and I asked you if you thought you could beat him.

You smiled, and quietly and confidently said to me, "Like the little train, I think I can." And you did!

When it comes to meeting the challenge of autism, I hope you will say, "I think I can."

> *I think you can.*

> *I think you will.*

> *I know you will!*

Love,
Pots